THE POETRY OF MOLYBDENUM

The Poetry of Molybdenum

Walter the Educator

SKB

Silent King Books a WhichHead Imprint

Copyright © 2023 by Walter the Educator

All rights reserved. No part of this book may be reproduced in any manner whatsoever without written permission except in the case of brief quotations embodied in critical articles and reviews.

First Printing, 2023

Disclaimer
This book is a literary work; poems are not about specific persons, locations, situations, and/or circumstances unless mentioned in a historical context. This book is for entertainment and informational purposes only. The author and publisher offer this information without warranties expressed or implied. No matter the grounds, neither the author nor the publisher will be accountable for any losses, injuries, or other damages caused by the reader's use of this book. The use of this book acknowledges an understanding and acceptance of this disclaimer.

"Earning a degree in chemistry changed my life!"
- Walter the Educator

dedicated to all the chemistry lovers, like myself, across the world

CONTENTS

Dedication v

Why I Created This Book? 1

One - Oh, Molybdenum 2

Two - Wonders It Store 4

Three - Forever In Awe 6

Four - We Rejoice 8

Five - Symbol Of Greatness 10

Six - Shining Bright 12

Seven - Essence Unfurled 14

Eight - Guardian Of Progress 16

Nine - Pillar Of Strength 18

Ten - Countless Ways 20

Eleven - A Catalyst True 22

Twelve - Symbolizing Resilience 24

Thirteen - Fuel Innovation 26

Fourteen - Vital Role 28

Fifteen - A Treasure We Cherish 30

Sixteen - Inspiration Finds Its Cue 32

Seventeen - Remarkable Ways 34

Eighteen - Leaving No Trace 36

Nineteen - Legacy Will Stay 38

Twenty - Cosmic Space 40

Twenty-One - Element Of Might 42

Twenty-Two - Day And Night 44

Twenty-Three - Technological Dream 46

Twenty-Four - Name That Rings 48

Twenty-Five - Reminder Of Life's
Kaleidoscope 50

Twenty-Six - We Intertwine 52

Twenty-Seven - Science And Steel 54

Twenty-Eight - Touch Every Soul 56

Twenty-Nine - A Story To Tell 58

Thirty - The Transformer 60

Thirty-One - Enduring And New 62

Thirty-Two - We Hail You 64

Thirty-Three - Hand In Hand 66

Thirty-Four - In All Its Forms 68

Thirty-Five - United By Molybdenum 70

About The Author 72

WHY I CREATED THIS BOOK?

Creating a poetry book about the chemical element of Molybdenum was a unique and intriguing experience. It allowed for a creative exploration of science, nature, and human emotions, merging the beauty of poetry with the fascinating properties of the element. By delving into the characteristics, history, and significance of Molybdenum, the poems can offer a fresh perspective on the world and our place in it. This book can also serve as a bridge between the arts and sciences, inspiring readers to appreciate the wonders of both disciplines.

ONE

OH, MOLYBDENUM

In the depths of the Earth's embrace,
Lies a treasure, a metal with grace.
Molybdenum, its name rings true,
A silent guardian, strong and true.

From ancient mines, it does emerge,
A symbol of strength, a noble surge.
With atomic number forty-two,
Its presence brings power anew.

A lustrous metal, silver and bright,
Infinite possibilities, like stars in the night.
An element, steadfast and bold,
Molybdenum, a story untold.

A catalyst, it helps reactions unfold,
In chemical realms, secrets it holds.
In steel's embrace, it finds its place,
Enhancing strength, with steady grace.

From industry to art, it finds its way,
A versatile element, every day.
In wires and rods, it's forged with might,
In engines and turbines, it shines so bright.
Molybdenum, a beacon in the dark,
A silent warrior, leaving its mark.
In the depths of the Earth, it quietly lies,
A symbol of resilience, reaching the skies.
Oh, Molybdenum, element divine,
Your presence, a treasure, so refined.
In the fabric of life, you weave your thread,
A testament to the wonders we tread.

TWO

WONDERS IT STORE

In the deep, dark Earth, a silent guardian resides,
Molybdenum, a symbol of strength and might.
With lustrous sheen, it sparkles in the night,
A treasure hidden, shining with pure light.

Molybdenum, oh element divine,
Unleashing power, like a sacred shrine.
Catalyzing reactions, its magic unwinds,
Unleashing potential, in infinite binds.

In the realm of steel, its strength does soar,
Forging creations, forever to endure.
From skyscrapers tall to ships that explore,
Molybdenum's touch, a legacy it ensures.

Versatile and mighty, in art it does show,
Brushstrokes of brilliance, a masterpiece to grow.

In engines it pulses, a fiery glow,
Molybdenum's presence, a force to bestow.
    Oh Molybdenum, hidden gem of Earth's core,
A beacon of resilience, forevermore.
Infinite possibilities, its essence does pour,
A divine element, life's wonders it store.

THREE

FOREVER IN AWE

    In the depths of nature's secret lair,
Where alchemy weaves its spell,
There lies a metal both strong and rare,
Molybdenum, its power to tell.
    A silent guardian, steadfast and true,
With a strength that never wanes,
Molybdenum, a symbol imbued,
With grace that forever remains.
    Beneath the earth's unwavering gaze,
It silently waits to be found,
A hidden treasure, a luminous blaze,
In the depths where wonders abound.
    From ancient times to the present day,
Molybdenum's worth holds true,
In every industry it finds its way,
Its versatility shining through.

A catalyst for change, it ignites,
Reactions that shape the world,
From steel to oil, its power delights,
As progress and innovation unfurled.

With resilience and might, it endures,
Unyielding to the tests of time,
Molybdenum, divine and pure,
A beacon of greatness, sublime.

So let us honor this element rare,
With gratitude and awe,
Molybdenum, beyond compare,
In our hearts, forever in awe.

FOUR

WE REJOICE

In the depths of Earth, a hidden might,
Unseen by many, yet shining bright,
Molybdenum, a guardian true,
A force of strength, both old and new.

Beneath the surface, it quietly dwells,
Within the rocks, where its story tells,
A catalyst for reactions grand,
Unleashing power at its command.

Its presence felt in steel so strong,
In bridges tall, it does belong,
A pillar of strength, unwavering and true,
Molybdenum, we owe much to you.

But beyond the steel, its talents abound,
In enzymes and proteins, it can be found,

A versatile element, it takes many forms,
Fueling life's processes, weathering storms.
    Oh, Molybdenum, you're a mystery untold,
A silent hero, both humble and bold,
Your atoms dance, igniting change,
In every corner, across the range.
    So let us honor this mighty element,
For its worth, its power, its pure intent,
Molybdenum, we raise our voice,
In awe of your presence, we rejoice.

FIVE

SYMBOL OF GREATNESS

In the realm of elements, strong and bold,
Lies Molybdenum, a tale yet untold.
A symbol of power, a force to behold,
With lustrous sheen, its story unfolds.

Born from the Earth, in its fiery core,
Molybdenum emerges, forevermore.
A catalyst of change, it sparks a reaction,
Igniting transformations with unwavering passion.

In alloys and steel, its presence is known,
Enhancing their strength, like a king on his throne.
Through heat and pressure, it remains unyielding,
A testament to resilience, forever revealing.

In the depths of industries, it finds its place,
A silent guardian, embracing every trace.

From oil refineries to nuclear might,
Molybdenum shines, casting its light.

In biological processes, it plays a part,
A hidden force, deep within the heart.
Enzymes rely on its touch, its caress,
Fueling life's processes, a divine finesse.

So let us celebrate this element grand,
Molybdenum, a treasure in our land.
With strength and power, it stands tall,
A symbol of greatness, for one and all.

SIX

SHINING BRIGHT

In the realm of elements, a noble one stands,
Molybdenum, versatile in its hands.
Symbol of Mo, it shines with might,
A metal of wonders, a brilliant light.

    Beneath the earth's surface, its secrets unfold,
Hidden treasures of silver and gold.
In mines deep and caverns wide,
Molybdenum's beauty can't be denied.

    A guardian of strength, it lends its aid,
In industries diverse, where it's well-played.
In steel's mighty heart, it adds its might,
Forging structures, sturdy and tight.

    A catalyst it becomes, in chemical reactions,
Guiding transformations, with precise actions.

In petroleum refining, it plays a role,
Breaking bonds, purifying the soul.

In the world of biology, it finds its way,
An enzyme's partner, a part to play.
Assisting life's processes, both great and small,
Molybdenum's presence, a gift to all.

Oh, Molybdenum, a symbol of grace,
A testament to nature's embrace.
From industry to life's intricate dance,
You shine, Molybdenum, in every chance.

So, let us celebrate this noble element,
In poetry and prose, its wonders lent.
For Molybdenum, a star in the night,
A gift from the cosmos, shining bright.

SEVEN

ESSENCE UNFURLED

In the heart of the Earth's embrace,
Molybdenum finds its rightful place.
A metal of strength and brilliant hue,
Its secrets unfold, revealing something new.

In factories and workshops, it takes the lead,
Forging the tools we all desperately need.
A catalyst for change, it sparks the fire,
In chemical reactions, it never tires.

Molybdenum, a guardian of steel,
In the heart of bridges, it makes them real.
With resilience unmatched, it holds the weight,
Defying gravity, an unyielding trait.

In jet engines roaring through the skies,
It withstands the heat, never compromises.

A protector of turbines, a force untamed,
Molybdenum's might, forever acclaimed.

But beyond the realm of industry's grasp,
It weaves its magic in nature's vast.
From plants to animals, it plays a role,
In enzymes and proteins, it takes control.

Molybdenum, a hidden treasure untold,
A symbol of progress and stories yet unfold.
In its atoms lie the secrets of life,
A guardian of progress, a steadfast rife.

So let us raise a toast to this element rare,
Molybdenum, a marvel beyond compare.
Infinite possibilities, its essence unfurled,
A testament to the wonders of our world.

EIGHT

GUARDIAN OF PROGRESS

In the realm of elements, Molybdenum stands tall,
A versatile metal, it outshines them all.
Resilient and steadfast, it never waivers,
In a world of change, it remains a savior.

From industry to nature, its presence is known,
In countless processes, its strength is shown.
Steel and alloys, it helps to fortify,
Building bridges and structures, reaching for the sky.

In the depths of the earth, where minerals dwell,
Molybdenum emerges, a story to tell.
A catalyst it becomes, in reactions so grand,
Transforming the ordinary into the extraordinary, hand in hand.

In petroleum refining, it plays a vital role,

Removing impurities, purifying the soul.
In turbines it protects, with a shield so strong,
Ensuring efficient energy, all day long.
    Oh, Molybdenum, your worth we adore,
A guardian of progress, forevermore.
From the depths of the earth to the heights of the sky,
Your presence never wanes, never says goodbye.

NINE

PILLAR OF STRENGTH

In the depths of the earth, a hidden treasure lies,
A metal of strength, where resilience resides.
Molybdenum, the guardian of progress and might,
Shining in the darkness, a beacon of light.

In the crucible of steel, it finds its place,
Forging the foundations with unwavering grace.
An alloy's companion, it lends its power,
Defying the flames, in the finest hour.

Through the fires of refinement, it emerges unscathed,
A catalyst for change, where progress is paved.
In the oil's embrace, it purifies the flow,
Removing impurities, letting energy grow.

Nature's humble friend, it journeys unseen,
A trace in the soil, where life's miracles glean.

From plants to animals, enzymes it fuels,
A vital ingredient, where health's secret rules.
    Molybdenum, a testament to endurance and might,
A symbol of greatness, shining so bright.
In every atom, its presence is known,
A silent guardian, forever it's grown.
    Oh, Molybdenum, element divine,
A gift to the world, so rare and fine.
In the tapestry of progress, you play your part,
A pillar of strength, forever in our hearts.

TEN

COUNTLESS WAYS

In the realm of elements, strong and true,
There lies a metal, bold and blue,
Molybdenum, its name resounds,
A force of nature, where strength abounds.
    In the depths of Earth, it finds its home,
A treasure hidden, yet not unknown,
Mining its depths, we bring it forth,
To shape our world, for better or worse.
    In factories and industries, it plays its part,
With properties that set it apart,
It tempers steel, with its mighty hold,
Forging structures, both new and old.
    From skyscrapers scraping the sky,
To bridges that gracefully defy,

Molybdenum stands tall and proud,
A testament to progress, strong and loud.
    But beyond the cities, it finds its grace,
In nature's realm, it finds its place,
Within enzymes, it sparks the fire,
Catalyzing reactions, never to tire.
    In the soil, it nurtures life,
Supporting plants, free from strife,
A vital nutrient, it helps them grow,
From seeds to blooms, a vibrant show.
    Molybdenum, a metal of might,
With strength and versatility, shining bright,
From industry to biology, it weaves its thread,
A symbol of progress, where life is fed.
    So let us celebrate, this element divine,
For the wonders it brings, in every line,
Molybdenum, we sing your praise,
A catalyst of change, in countless ways.

ELEVEN

A CATALYST TRUE

In the depths of the Earth, a treasure lies,
A metal strong, with brilliance in its guise.
Molybdenum, guardian of progress untold,
A hidden power, a story yet unfold.

In the fires of industry, it takes its place,
Refining, strengthening, with every trace.
From steel to turbines, it lends its might,
Transforming raw materials into shining light.

A catalyst of change, it sparks the flame,
Unleashing reactions, never to be the same.
With bonds unyielding, it forges new paths,
Guiding us forward, overcoming life's wraths.

In enzymes, it dwells, a secret divine,
Fueling life's processes, in every design.

From nitrogen fixation to detoxification,
Molybdenum's essence, the source of creation.
    A silent hero, it silently thrives,
In chemistry's realm, where knowledge derives.
A symbol of strength, resilience, and more,
Molybdenum, the element we adore.
    So let us celebrate this mighty name,
For it is Molybdenum that fuels our flame.
A guardian of progress, a catalyst true,
In every endeavor, it sees us through.

TWELVE

SYMBOLIZING RESILIENCE

In the depths of the Earth, a treasure lies,
A metal of strength, where secrets arise.
Molybdenum, a name both bold and grand,
A catalyst of change, a guiding hand.

In the realm of industry, it takes its place,
Refining petroleum with its grace.
Through pipes and valves, it flows with might,
Purifying fuels, igniting the night.

In turbines it spins, a force so vast,
Harnessing power, forever steadfast.
With heat and motion, it drives the land,
A symbol of progress, a future unplanned.

In nature's realm, it finds its way,
Within enzymes, proteins, a vital array.

A nutrient for plants, it fosters growth,
From earth to sky, its power shows.
    Endurance and strength, it does possess,
A metal revered, it won't acquiesce.
Transforming reactions with every touch,
Molybdenum's presence, it means so much.
    Oh, Molybdenum, a beacon of light,
Catalyzing change, with all its might.
In chemistry's realm, it shines so bright,
Symbolizing resilience, knowledge's delight.

THIRTEEN

FUEL INNOVATION

In the realms of industry, you shine so bright,
Molybdenum, a symbol of strength and might.
With steel as your canvas, you paint a new dawn,
Forging the future, as progress marches on.

    Beneath the earth's surface, where secrets reside,
You rest in the soil, with grace and with pride.
Nature's own creation, a gift from the core,
A treasure so precious, forever we adore.

    In enzymes and proteins, you weave your design,
A catalyst of life, a force so divine.
From nitrogen fixation to sulfur reduction,
You fuel the reactions, with boundless instruction.

    Your power to resist, to endure and withstand,
Is a testament to your resilience, so grand.

In extreme conditions, you thrive and you grow,
A beacon of hope, where few dare to go.
    Molybdenum, a conductor of change,
A metal with purpose, so vast and so strange.
From airplanes to turbines, your presence is felt,
A driving force, where progress is dealt.
    So let us raise our voices, in praise and in song,
To Molybdenum, a symbol so strong.
For in your essence, we find inspiration,
To push past limits, and fuel innovation.

FOURTEEN

VITAL ROLE

In the depths of the Earth, where secrets lie,
A metal of strength, Molybdenum, they sigh.
With atomic number forty-two, it stands tall,
A symbol of progress, in industries enthralled.

In steel, it lends its might, its power untold,
Forging structures sturdy, unyielding and bold.
From bridges to ships, skyscrapers so high,
Molybdenum's presence, it cannot be denied.

In catalysts it thrives, a chemical dance,
Unlocking reactions, a magical trance.
From oil refineries to chemical plants,
Molybdenum's touch, a catalyst that enchants.

But beyond the factories and the bustling mills,
Molybdenum's significance, nature reveals.

In enzymes, it participates, a vital role,
Supporting life's processes, a gift to behold.

From nitrogen fixation to detoxification,
Molybdenum's enzymes, a marvel of creation.
In the soil, it helps plants to grow,
Nurturing life, a secret it does bestow.

So let us celebrate this element divine,
Molybdenum, a treasure in every line.
From industry to nature, it weaves its spell,
A symbol of resilience, it will always compel.

FIFTEEN

A TREASURE WE CHERISH

In the depths of earth, a treasure did lie,
A metal rare, with strength to defy.
Molybdenum, a name quite unique,
A symbol of might, its power we seek.

In industry's grasp, it finds its place,
Forging steel with a resolute grace.
Its strength unmatched, it withstands the heat,
Transforming the ordinary into elite.

Catalyst supreme, it sparks the flame,
Igniting reactions, without any shame.
From oil's dark slumber, it purifies,
Unveiling the purity that underlies.

But beyond the factories and refining towers,
In the realm of life, its true worth flowers.

Enzymes it aids, in each living cell,
A vital nutrient, where life's stories dwell.

In the soil it resides, a silent guide,
Nurturing plants, with a love deep and wide.
From the greenest meadows to the tallest trees,
Molybdenum's touch, brings life to its knees.

Oh Molybdenum, element divine,
A symbol of progress, a beacon to shine.
Endurance and might, your essence portrays,
Innovation's ally, guiding our ways.

So let us celebrate, this metal so grand,
For in its presence, we firmly stand.
Molybdenum, a treasure we cherish,
In our hearts forever, it shall never perish.

SIXTEEN

INSPIRATION FINDS ITS CUE

In nature's realm, where life finds its way,
A catalyst of change, Molybdenum holds sway.
An element rare, a metal with might,
It sparks reactions, unveiling nature's light.

In the depths of the ocean, where darkness resides,
Molybdenum awakens life, where the abyss hides.
It breathes in the depths, where no sunlight gleams,
Fueling the flames of existence, in unseen streams.

In the forge of chemistry, where bonds are forged,
Molybdenum stands strong, its strength never torched.
Resilient and steadfast, it withstands the test,
Transforming compounds, with its catalytic zest.

In industry's embrace, where progress takes flight,
Molybdenum stands tall, a beacon of might.

From steel's core to engines' roar,
It fuels innovation, forevermore.

In enzymes and proteins, where life takes form,
Molybdenum nurtures, a protector from harm.
It guides the reactions, with precision and grace,
Breathing life into molecules, in an intricate embrace.

In the garden of life, where plants find their might,
Molybdenum whispers, igniting their light.
A nutrient essential, it fosters their growth,
A gardener's companion, nurturing the oath.

Oh, Molybdenum, symbol of resilience and might,
In your essence, nature's secrets take flight.
A catalyst, a strength, a nurturer true,
In your presence, inspiration finds its cue.

SEVENTEEN

REMARKABLE WAYS

In the realm of elements, a jewel does shine,
Its name is Molybdenum, a force so fine.
Fueling innovation, it sparks the fire,
Igniting ambition, taking us higher.

In enzymes and proteins, it finds its home,
Guiding reactions, where life's secrets roam.
A nutrient for plants, a gift from above,
Nurturing growth, with a touch of love.

Resilient and mighty, it stands tall and strong,
A symbol of power, it carries along.
A catalyst for change, it leads the way,
Transforming the mundane, day after day.

In the garden of life, it whispers and nurtures,
A guardian, protector from harm's cruel suture.

A companion to the gardener, steadfast and true,
Molybdenum, we owe our gratitude to you.

Oh, element of wonders, you inspire with light,
A beacon of hope, shining through the night.
From industry to nature, your presence does bloom,
Molybdenum, you illuminate our world's gloom.

So let us celebrate this element grand,
With its shimmering brilliance, across the land.
Molybdenum, oh Molybdenum, we sing your praise,
Forever grateful for your remarkable ways.

EIGHTEEN

LEAVING NO TRACE

In the depths of Earth, a hidden treasure lies,
A metal rare, with strength that never dies.
Molybdenum, the element of boundless might,
Embraces industries, shining ever so bright.

From steel to aerospace, its touch is profound,
Forging bridges, skyscrapers that astound.
In the heart of turbines, it spins with grace,
Harnessing energy, powering the human race.

In nature's realm, where life begins to bloom,
Molybdenum whispers secrets, dispelling gloom.
A catalyst for plants, it breathes life anew,
Nurturing the soil, painting the world in hues.

In laboratories, where innovation thrives,
Molybdenum guides reactions, as nature strives.
Catalyzing progress, fueling our dreams,
Unleashing brilliance through its gleaming streams.

Transcending boundaries, it transforms with grace,
Inspiring minds to reach a higher place.
Molybdenum, a luminary in our world,
Unleashes potential, like a flag unfurled.

Now, without images, let words alone convey,
Molybdenum's leadership, lighting the way.
A beacon of hope, it shines in darkest night,
Igniting possibilities, igniting our fight.

Molybdenum, a symbol of strength and might,
Leading us forward, with its radiant light.
In unity we stand, embracing its embrace,
For Molybdenum guides us, leaving no trace.

NINETEEN

LEGACY WILL STAY

In the depths of Earth's embrace, Molybdenum resides,
A silent catalyst, where innovation abides.
With strength and resilience, it fuels the forge,
Igniting progress, where dreams take their surge.

From the laboratories to the factories' gleam,
Molybdenum dances, a conductor supreme.
In alloys and steels, its presence is felt,
Forging the future, where wonders are dealt.

Beneath the moon's gaze, in the garden of life,
Molybdenum blossoms, banishing strife.
Nurturing growth, it whispers with grace,
A beacon of hope, in every sacred space.

From enzymes to proteins, life's intricate dance,
Molybdenum weaves, a mystical trance.

A catalyst for change, it breathes life anew,
Unleashing potential, where dreams can accrue.

In the tapestry of progress, it takes the lead,
A symbol of resilience, in times of need.
A guardian of transformation, it stands tall,
Guiding us forward, inspiring one and all.

Oh, Molybdenum, your presence divine,
A symbol of greatness, where marvels align.
Through innovation and growth, you pave the way,
In our hearts forever, your legacy will stay.

TWENTY

COSMIC SPACE

In the depths of Earth's embrace, where secrets lie untold,
There dwells a mighty element, a tale yet to unfold.
Molybdenum, oh noble one, with strength and grace adorned,
A guardian of reactions, where life's mysteries are formed.

Within the enzymes of life, you play a vital role,
Catalyzing transformations, as nature takes its toll.
From nitrogen to nitrates, you guide the way with might,
Nurturing the soil, where greenest fields take flight.

In the fires of industry, your presence brings forth light,
Transforming raw materials, igniting progress's might.

From steel to superalloys, you shape the world we see,
A beacon of innovation, inspiring industry.

Oh Molybdenum, you're more than just a name,
A symbol of potential, a catalyst for change.
From shining stars up high, to oceans vast and deep,
Your touch brings forth wonders, where dreams and hope shall seep.

So let us raise our voices, in praise of your might,
For you, Molybdenum, are a guiding star at night.
From chemistry to nature's reign, your essence we embrace,
A pillar of transformation, in this vast cosmic space.

TWENTY-ONE

ELEMENT OF MIGHT

In the depths of Earth, a treasure lies,
A metal rare, with boundless ties.
Molybdenum, a name so grand,
A catalyst for dreams, a guiding hand.

In the forge of time, where progress thrives,
Molybdenum sparks, as ambition strives.
With strength untold and resilience pure,
It nurtures growth, a steadfast allure.

From ancient soils to modern skies,
Molybdenum's presence never dies.
A symbol of transformation, it shines bright,
Igniting possibilities, a beacon of light.

In industry's embrace, it finds its place,
Forging paths of innovation, with grace.

From steel to glass, it lends its might,
Shaping the world, with a radiant sight.
    Unyielding and steadfast, it stands tall,
A catalyst of change, inspiring all.
In laboratories and factories, it weaves,
Advancing knowledge, fulfilling needs.
    Oh Molybdenum, element divine,
Your essence transcends the sands of time.
A symbol of potential, a force untamed,
In every aspect of life, your legacy's claimed.
    So let us cherish this metal rare,
With gratitude and awe, let us declare,
Molybdenum, the element of might,
A catalyst for progress, shining bright.

TWENTY-TWO

DAY AND NIGHT

In the depths of Earth, a treasure lies,
A gleaming metal, a wondrous prize,
Molybdenum, a catalyst of dreams,
Igniting progress with its fiery beams.

In factories tall, where steel is made,
Molybdenum stands, unyielding, unswayed,
For it strengthens the bonds of iron and steel,
Forging structures that will never yield.

In the heart of the glassblower's art,
Molybdenum plays its supportive part,
With its melting point high and true,
It molds molten glass, a masterpiece anew.

But beyond the realms of industry's might,
Molybdenum dances in nature's light,

It weaves its magic in the soil and air,
Nurturing life with its tender care.

From enzymes to proteins, it lends a hand,
Guiding reactions, a maestro grand,
Fueling the engines of life's grand design,
A silent hero, both humble and kind.

So let us celebrate this metal divine,
A symbol of strength, a radiant sign,
Molybdenum, we honor your might,
For you fuel our dreams, day and night.

TWENTY-THREE

TECHNOLOGICAL DREAM

In the realm of industry, you shine bright,
Molybdenum, a metal of sheer might.
With strength unmatched, you forge a path,
Transforming the world with your fiery wrath.
From steel to turbines, you lend your grace,
Harnessing power, in every place.
Your presence felt in every machine,
A catalyst for progress, a technological dream.
From skyscrapers high to bridges strong,
Molybdenum, you right every wrong.
Your resilience and tenacity,
Shape our world with audacity.
In factories and laboratories,
You fuel innovation, setting minds free.

Catalyzing reactions, driving discovery,
Molybdenum, you're the key to our recovery.
 Oh, mighty element, so versatile,
Your impact on industry, impossible to defile.
From the depths of the Earth to the stars above,
Molybdenum, you're a beacon of love.
 So let us celebrate your wondrous might,
Molybdenum, shining star of the night.
In the realm of industry, you'll always be,
A symbol of progress, for all to see.

TWENTY-FOUR

NAME THAT RINGS

In the depths of Earth's embrace, behold,
A metal rare, a story yet untold.
Molybdenum, a name that rings,
With strength and grace, it spreads its wings.

A catalyst, it sparks the flame,
Igniting progress in its own name.
In laboratories, it takes its place,
Guiding scientists in their cosmic chase.

A symbol of potential, it shines bright,
A guiding star in the grandest night.
With atomic number forty-two,
Molybdenum, we turn to you.

In nature's realm, you quietly reside,
Amongst minerals, where secrets hide.
From mountains high to valleys deep,
Your presence in ores, a treasure to keep.

In industry, you play your part,
Transforming raw materials with your art.
In steel's embrace, you lend your might,
Forging structures, sturdy and tight.

  Resilient and enduring, you stand tall,
A silent hero, above all.
Molybdenum, you shape the world,
Unveiling wonders, unfurled.

  So let us celebrate this noble element,
A beacon of progress, so heaven-sent.
Molybdenum, we sing your praise,
For in your presence, innovation stays.

TWENTY-FIVE

REMINDER OF LIFE'S KALEIDOSCOPE

In the heart of mines, a treasure lies,
A noble element that never dies.
Molybdenum, strong and pure,
A metal that will endure.

In the depths of Earth, where darkness dwells,
Molybdenum's story silently tells.
From humble beginnings, it emerged,
With strength and resilience, it surged.

In the fires of industry, it finds its place,
A catalyst of progress, with grace.
From steel to electronics, it lends its might,
Molybdenum shines, a beacon of light.

In the laboratory, chemists explore,
The secrets of Molybdenum they adore.

Its atomic structure, a marvel to behold,
Unlocking mysteries, untold.

In nature's realm, Molybdenum thrives,
A silent force, where life derives.
From enzymes to plants, its touch profound,
In every corner, its presence is found.

Oh, Molybdenum, we sing your praise,
For all the wonders you amaze.
A symbol of innovation, a vessel of change,
In our world, you rearrange.

So let us celebrate, this element rare,
Molybdenum, beyond compare.
For in your essence, we find hope,
A reminder of life's kaleidoscope.

TWENTY-SIX

WE INTERTWINE

In the realm of industry, strong and steadfast,
A metal emerges, Molybdenum unsurpassed.
With its gleaming presence, it takes its place,
A catalyst of progress, with elegance and grace.

In the fires of innovation, it finds its home,
Forging the future, where possibilities roam.
From skyscrapers soaring to the heavens above,
To the depths of machines, where gears interweave.

Molybdenum, a symbol of strength and might,
In factories and workshops, a guiding light.
Its resistance to heat, a shield so bold,
In furnaces and reactors, its secrets unfold.

As the Earth's hidden treasure, it resides,
In mines and mountains, where mystery hides.

A guardian of nature, it nurtures the land,
Feeding the soil with its nurturing hand.
  From ancient times to modern days,
Molybdenum's story, forever ablaze.
A symbol of transformation, it stands,
Shaping our world, with skilled hands.
  Oh Molybdenum, we sing your praise,
For the wonders you bring, in countless ways.
In industry and nature, you leave your mark,
A shining beacon, lighting up the dark.
  So, let us celebrate this element divine,
For its resilience and power, we intertwine.
Molybdenum, we raise our voice,
In awe of your essence, we rejoice.

TWENTY-SEVEN

SCIENCE AND STEEL

In the depths of Earth, a hidden gem,
A metal strong, a brilliant emblem.
Molybdenum, with its lustrous grace,
Unveils its secrets, a rare embrace.

Forged in the heart of ancient stars,
It traveled far, from cosmic scars.
Nature's alchemist, with powers untold,
Molybdenum, a tale to unfold.

From mines it emerges, steadfast and pure,
A symbol of strength, enduring and sure.
In industry, it finds its purpose grand,
A catalyst for progress, at its command.

In steel, it fortifies, with resilience profound,
Endowing structures, unyielding and sound.

In engines it dances, a flame's fiery gleam,
Igniting innovation, a visionary's dream.

From towering skyscrapers to bridges that span,
Molybdenum shapes the world, with its mighty plan.
A conductor of heat, a guardian of light,
It illuminates pathways, in the darkest of night.

Yet beyond the realm of science and steel,
Molybdenum's essence, it reveals.
A metaphor for life, a transformative force,
Unveiling potential, on a cosmic course.

So let us celebrate this element rare,
Molybdenum, beyond compare.
A symbol of progress, a beacon of might,
Guiding humanity, towards a future bright.

TWENTY-EIGHT

TOUCH EVERY SOUL

In the realm of industry, bold and strong,
Lies a metal, a treasure, Molybdenum.
With a luster that shines, like the sun's golden ray,
It paves the path for innovation's way.

In factories and workshops, it takes its stand,
Forging machines, with a masterful hand.
From skyscrapers tall, to bridges so grand,
Molybdenum's might, it helps them withstand.

In engines it thrives, where heat is intense,
Unyielding, unwavering, it shows its resilience.
Catalyst it becomes, for chemical reactions,
Igniting the spark of scientific attractions.

Its presence is silent, yet it shapes us all,
From the buildings we admire, to the cars that enthral.

A symbol of strength, an element of might,
Molybdenum's power, shines ever so bright.
   So let us celebrate this versatile friend,
Whose impact on industry knows no end.
Molybdenum, we honor your role,
As you shape the world, and touch every soul.

TWENTY-NINE

A STORY TO TELL

In the depths of the earth where secrets lie,
There dwells a metal, radiant and sly.
Molybdenum, sturdy and bold,
A tale of transformation, yet untold.

From the mines it emerges, a hidden gem,
An alchemist's dream, a precious stem.
Its atomic dance, a symphony of might,
Unleashing wonders, a dazzling light.

In industry's embrace, it finds its role,
A catalyst of progress, an agent of control.
Steel's companion, it strengthens the core,
Forging bridges, skyscrapers, and more.

A warrior of heat, it withstands the flame,
In furnaces ablaze, it claims its fame.
Tempering the elements, it stands tall,
Defying limits, it conquers all.

In nature's embrace, it weaves its tale,
In leaves of green, it sparks and prevails.
A vital trace in every living cell,
Enriching life's tapestry, a story to tell.
 Molybdenum, symbol of resilience and grace,
A testament to the human race.
From earth to sky, it guides our quest,
Unveiling the future, we are truly blessed.

THIRTY

THE TRANSFORMER

In the depths of Earth's embrace, Molybdenum resides,
A hidden gem, a secret force, where strength and progress collide.
Amidst the rocks and ores it dwells, a silent hero unfurled,
Transforming the world with its might, a gift to all the world.

   In nature's realm, it forms its home, in minerals, it's found,
A shimmering essence, steadfast and profound.
From mountains tall to valleys wide, it weaves its magic thread,
Binding atoms with resilience, where dreams and hopes are bred.

In industry's embrace, it shines, a beacon of innovation,
Forging bridges, buildings tall, a testament to creation.
With steel it dances, hand in hand, imparting strength and might,
Fueling progress, shaping cities, a symbol of human light.

In labs and scientific minds, it sparks a wondrous fire,
Advancing knowledge, breaking barriers, pushing ever higher.
From catalysts to enzymes, it breathes life into cells,
Unleashing nature's secrets, where science's story dwells.

Molybdenum, the mighty, a catalyst of change,
A symbol of resilience, a world it rearranges.
With every bond it forms, it whispers of a brighter day,
Guiding us towards a future where progress will hold sway.

So let us celebrate this element, this silent guiding star,
For Molybdenum's might, its power, will eternally endure,
A testament to human will, a legacy to impart,
Molybdenum, the transformer, forever in our heart.

THIRTY-ONE

ENDURING AND NEW

In the depths of the earth, a hidden gem,
Lies Molybdenum, a metal to condemn.
With strength and resilience, it stands tall,
A catalyst for change, it impacts us all.

In nature's embrace, its presence is found,
In minerals and ores, deep underground.
A companion to copper, it adds strength and might,
In alloys and steels, shining in the light.

In industry, its influence is vast,
From oil refineries to airplanes that blast.
A guardian of heat, it resists corrosion,
In high-temperature applications, it's a trusted companion.

From skyscrapers towering above the ground,
To bridges that span with a mighty sound,

Molybdenum's strength, unwavering and true,
Supports structures, enduring and new.

In labs and research, it plays a key role,
A catalyst for science, it unlocks the soul.
From chemical reactions to catalytic converters,
Molybdenum's impact, forever it hovers.

With transformative power, it shapes the future,
A symbol of progress, forever it nurtures.
As we marvel at its versatility and might,
Molybdenum, a metal that shines so bright.

So let us celebrate this element profound,
Molybdenum, a treasure that can be found.
In nature, industry, and scientific endeavor,
It stands as a testament, forever and ever.

THIRTY-TWO

WE HAIL YOU

In the realm where elements dance and twirl,
There shines a metal, Molybdenum, a precious pearl.
With strength unmatched, it forges its way,
A symbol of resilience, come what may.

    In nature's embrace, it plays a vital role,
Enriching soils, nurturing life as a whole.
Catalyst of enzymes, a chemical key,
Unlocking the secrets of life's mystery.

    In industry's grasp, it finds its place,
A cornerstone of progress, with unwavering grace.
From skyscrapers tall to bridges so grand,
Molybdenum's might, an architect's hand.

    In laboratories gleaming, scientists explore,
Its properties unique, forever they adore.

In alloys and steels, it adds strength and might,
Forging a future, shining bright.
    Molybdenum, a beacon of change,
Innovation's ally, it knows no range.
Transforming the world, shaping our fate,
In its presence, greatness we create.
    Oh, Molybdenum, element divine,
Your essence, a testament, forever will shine.
A symbol of power, in every form,
Molybdenum, we hail you, and your transformative norm.

THIRTY-THREE

HAND IN HAND

In the depths of Earth, where treasures lie,
A shimmering element catches the eye.
Molybdenum, strong and true,
A symbol of progress, it shines through.

In industries vast, its worth is known,
From steel to turbines, its power is shown.
A catalyst for strength, it does provide,
Enhancing materials far and wide.

In aerospace, it soars and flies,
Resilient and durable, it defies the skies.
From engines to wings, it lends its might,
Guiding us forward, like a beacon of light.

In chemistry labs, its secrets unfold,
Aiding reactions, transforming gold.

A catalyst supreme, it speeds the way,
Unleashing potential, day by day.

In technology's realm, it takes the lead,
With heat resistance, it meets our need.
From electronics to solar arrays,
Molybdenum paves the path of brighter days.

Oh, Molybdenum, element divine,
Your versatility, truly sublime.
A symbol of progress, a force so grand,
With you, we shape the future, hand in hand.

THIRTY-FOUR

IN ALL ITS FORMS

In the realm of strength and steel,
There lies a metal, mighty and real.
Molybdenum, its name resounds,
A symbol of power that knows no bounds.

    Within its atoms, secrets unfold,
A story of resilience, untold.
From the depths of Earth, it does arise,
To shape the world with its silent cries.

    In construction, it stands tall and true,
Supporting structures, old and new.
Bridging gaps, forging connections,
Molybdenum, the architect's reflections.

    In industry, it's a force to reckon,
Enhancing alloys, forging weapons.

With steely resolve, it withstands,
The heat and pressure of man's demands.
    In the laboratory, it sparks innovation,
Unveiling truths through experimentation.
A catalyst for scientific endeavor,
Molybdenum, the researcher's treasure.
    In the realm of technology, it prevails,
Powering engines, blazing trails.
From aerospace to electronics grand,
Molybdenum, the engineer's guiding hand.
    Oh, Molybdenum, you shine so bright,
A beacon of progress, a guiding light.
Through your might, the world transforms,
Unleashing potential, in all its forms.

THIRTY-FIVE

UNITED BY MOLYBDENUM

In the depths of the Earth, a treasure untold,
A gleaming metal, Molybdenum, bold.
A catalyst of change, it silently resides,
Unleashing its power, where progress presides.

    In laboratories, its secrets unfold,
Aiding in reactions, as discoveries are sold.
A catalyst of science, it plays its part,
Unlocking new realms, igniting the heart.

    With strength unyielding, it weathers the storm,
A pillar of resilience, sturdy and warm.
In construction's embrace, it stands tall and proud,
Enduring the test of time, unbowed.

    In industries vast, it finds its due,
Forging new pathways, creating anew.

From engines to turbines, technologies thrive,
Harnessing Molybdenum, keeping dreams alive.
   Through the lens of chemistry, it reveals,
A world of compounds, where innovation appeals.
A catalyst of transformation, it wields its might,
Shaping the future, in a blinding light.
   Molybdenum, a symbol of progress, you see,
A guiding force, inspiring humanity.
With each discovery, a step we ascend,
United by Molybdenum, our journey will never end.

ABOUT THE AUTHOR

Walter the Educator is one of the pseudonyms for Walter Anderson. Formally educated in Chemistry, Business, and Education, he is an educator, an author, a diverse entrepreneur, and he is the son of a disabled war veteran. "Walter the Educator" shares his time between educating and creating. He holds interests and owns several creative projects that entertain, enlighten, enhance, and educate, hoping to inspire and motivate you.

Follow, find new works, and stay up to date
with Walter the Educator™
at WaltertheEducator.com

www.ingramcontent.com/pod-product-compliance
Lightning Source LLC
LaVergne TN
LVHW051959060526
838201LV00059B/3737